IF YOU WERE A KID SURVIVING A
Hurricane

BY JOSH GREGORY • ILLUSTRATED BY KELLY KENNEDY

CHILDREN'S PRESS® An Imprint of Scholastic Inc.

Content Consultant
Deanna Hence, PhD, Assistant Professor, Department of Atmospheric Sciences,
University of Illinois at Urbana-Champaign, Champaign, Illinois

NOTE TO THE READER, PARENT, LIBRARIAN, AND TEACHER: This book combines a historical fiction
narrative with nonfiction fact boxes. While all the nonfiction fact boxes are historically accurate
and true, the fiction comes solely from the imaginations of the author and illustrator.

Photos ©: 9: Harvepino/iStock/Getty Images; 11: Mikkel Juul Jensen/Science Source; 13: Science Source; 15: Mark
Elias/Bloomberg/Getty Images; 19: Dreammediapeel/Dreamstime; 21: Mario Tama/Getty Images; 23: Rusty Kennedy/
AP Images; 25: Cultura RM Exclusive/Jason Persoff Stormdoctor/Getty Images; 27: PacificCoastNews/Newscom.

Library of Congress Cataloging-in-Publication Data
Names: Gregory, Josh. | Kennedy, Kelly (Illustrator)
Title: If you were a kid surviving a hurricane / by Josh Gregory ; illustrated by Kelly Kennedy.
Description: New York, NY : Children's Press, an imprint of Scholastic Inc., [2018] | Series: If you were a kid |
Includes bibliographical references and index.
Identifiers: LCCN 2016054371| ISBN 9780531237458 (library binding) | ISBN 9780531239469 (pbk.)
Subjects: LCSH: Hurricanes—Juvenile literature. | Severe storms—Juvenile literature.
Classification: LCC QC944.2 .G7394 2018 | DDC 551.55/2—dc23
LC record available at https://lccn.loc.gov/2016054371

3 4 5 6 7 8 9 10 R 27 26 25 24 23 22 21 20 19 18
Scholastic Inc., 557 Broadway, New York, NY 10012.

TABLE OF CONTENTS

A Different Way of Life

Every year, about 100 huge storms called tropical cyclones form above oceans around the world. As the winds in these storms move faster and faster, the storms can turn into hurricanes. They sometimes start moving toward land. When they arrive in areas where people live, flooding and wind can be devastating. Buildings may be destroyed. Trees are often ripped out of the ground. In the strongest storms, cars can be thrown through the air like toys. People might be hurt or even killed. Many people leave their homes and head away from the coast when hurricanes are expected to hit. But not everyone escapes. Some people don't have anywhere to go. Others simply don't want to leave.

Turn the page to visit a coastal city as a hurricane is on its way. You will see that trying to survive a hurricane can be a scary experience.

Meet Carrie!

This is Carrie Robinson. She loves to read books and learn new things. Recently, she has been reading a lot about hurricanes. She heard that one is heading toward her town, and she is scared. Her parents insist that everything will be fine. They have lived through hurricanes before. They don't think this one will be any different . . .

Meet Dan!

This is Dan Lopez. He lives with his grandma and his very best friend: a small, brown-and-white dog named Teddy. But Teddy has been missing since yesterday. Dan can't find him anywhere in the neighborhood. He knows the storm is on its way, and he is worried about his furry little friend . . .

Carrie looked up from her book to watch the news report on TV. "Once again, the mayor has called for an **evacuation**," said the newscaster. "Everyone should leave town and head north." Carrie's parents were busy making breakfast. They didn't seem to be paying attention to the TV.

"Did you hear that?" Carrie asked. "Shouldn't we leave?"

Carrie's dad chuckled. "Don't worry," he said. "We'll be okay."

HOW DOES A HURRICANE FORM?

A hurricane forms as air that is heated by warm ocean water moves upward. The surrounding air moves in to fill the space the hot air left behind. As this new air warms, it also moves upward. Moisture in the warm air forms clouds. Wind and Earth's rotation cause the clouds to spin in a spiral. With enough wind and warm air, these clouds can spin faster and faster. Once the wind speed reaches 74 miles per hour (119 kilometers per hour) the storm is considered a hurricane.

Seen from above, it is easy to spot a hurricane's swirling shape.

A few blocks away, Dan walked down the sidewalk with flyers announcing his lost dog. Every couple of blocks, he stopped to call out Teddy's name. As he searched for the dog, he noticed that the neighborhood was quiet. A few people were putting boards over their windows. Others were building walls out of sandbags. However, most of the neighbors seemed to have left town.

LOST DOG

A LOOK INSIDE A HURRICANE

Scientists divide hurricanes into three sections. The center is called the eye. Here, everything is calm. There is no wind or rain. Surrounding the eye is the eyewall. It is made of fast-moving clouds. This is the part of the storm with the strongest wind and rain. Around the eyewall are rain bands. Here, wind and rain decrease as they get farther from the eye.

This diagram shows the three main parts of a hurricane.

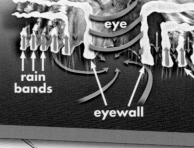

eye

rain bands

eyewall

rain bands

That evening, Carrie sat by her bedroom window and watched the wind blowing outside. She was growing more worried by the hour. The streets were empty. Everyone was gone or indoors. Suddenly, a small dog popped into view. What was he doing outdoors? Carrie ran outside to see whom he belonged to. As she got close, the dog ran away. "Wait!" she said. "Come back!" Forgetting her fear of the storm, she chased after him.

WHAT'S IN A NAME?

Every hurricane is named with a common human name. This is done to avoid confusion. By giving storms short, easy-to-remember names, it is less likely that people will get them mixed up. Even when two storms are going on at the same time, scientists and other weather experts can easily communicate about what is happening with each one.

The hurricane that devastated the Gulf Coast in August 2005 was named Katrina.

Grandma had cooked a delicious dinner, but Dan just wasn't hungry. All day long, he had looked for Teddy. The dog was nowhere to be found. Dan's grandma saw the sadness in his face. She tried to comfort him.

"Teddy will be fine," she said. "He's been lost before. He always finds his way home." But she knew this time was different. A dangerous storm was drawing near.

PREDICTING A HURRICANE

Meteorologists keep a close eye on all tropical storms that form. These scientists use **satellites**, computers, and other technology to watch storms grow and track their movements. This helps them predict when and where a hurricane might reach land. They release warnings to let people know when storms are coming.

A meteorologist tracks a hurricane's movement on a map.

As Dan glanced out the window at the worsening weather, he was surprised to see a girl running toward the front door. He got up and opened the door to see what she wanted. As he did, Teddy darted into the house at top speed.

"You found Teddy!" he said with a huge smile.

Carrie nodded. She was out of breath from running.

"You kids better get inside," Dan's grandma said. "Things are looking bad out there."

MEASURING A STORM'S STRENGTH

The strength of a hurricane is measured by its wind speed. Meteorologists use five categories to describe hurricanes. This is called the Saffir-Simpson Hurricane Wind Scale. All five categories are dangerous. However, storms in Category 3 or higher are considered "major" hurricanes.

Category	Wind Speeds
1	74–95 miles per hour (119–153 kph)
2	96–110 miles per hour (154–177 kph)
3	111–129 miles per hour (178–208 kph)
4	130–156 miles per hour (209–251 kph)
5	157 miles per hour (252 kph) or higher

Carrie realized that she had run a long way from home.

"You should call your parents," said Dan's grandma. "Tell them you're staying here."

Carrie didn't want to stay with strangers. But Dan and his grandma seemed really nice, and the storm was coming quickly. She got out her phone and dialed home. Her parents were upset that she had run off on her own, but they told her to stay put at Dan's house.

STORM SURGE

Wind isn't a hurricane's only danger. Rising water is also a big problem. As a hurricane moves toward land, it pushes ocean water forward. This is called a storm surge. It causes the water level to rise very quickly at the coastline. Huge waves can crash onto land. These waves and rising water levels can destroy buildings and flood entire cities.

Water slams against a storm barrier in Rhode Island during Hurricane Irene in 2011.

It was hard to sleep that night. Not long after dozing off, noise from outside woke Carrie and Dan. Looking out the window, the kids saw trees whipping around in the wind. Rain poured down in sheets. Worst of all, the streets were starting to flood.

Dan shook his grandma awake. He pointed toward the rapidly rising waters outside. "What should we do?" he asked.

A WALL AGAINST WATER

In places where hurricanes are common, people build many defenses. Areas such as the Gulf Coast and South Florida rely on **levees** for protection. These are walls that keep ocean water from flooding the land. Many levees are made of dirt or rocks. In some areas, stronger levees are built with concrete or even metal.

Workers make repairs to levees in New Orleans, Louisiana, in 2006 after Hurricane Katrina.

"Head upstairs!" Dan's grandma shouted.

Water was beginning to seep into the house.

The water rose quickly. Soon, even the second story of the house was partially underwater. Everyone climbed into the attic. But even that wasn't safe from the flood. As the sun rose, Dan helped his grandma and Carrie climb out a window and onto the roof. The rain had finally stopped, but the whole neighborhood was underwater.

CITIES UNDERWATER

The combination of storm surge and heavy rain can cause serious flooding during a hurricane. This is often the most dangerous part of the storm. For example, 56 people died when Hurricane Floyd hit the East Coast of the United States in 1999. Fifty of these deaths were caused by flooding. People drown or become trapped in buildings. Because roads are underwater, rescue workers cannot reach the victims.

A school bus in Pennsylvania is submerged by floodwaters during Hurricane Floyd in 1999.

Everyone was cold and frightened. They didn't know what would happen next. But then Carrie spotted something moving toward them. As it came closer, she realized it was her family's fishing boat. Her parents had come to the rescue!

"I'm sorry we didn't listen to you about the storm," her dad said as he helped everyone onto the boat. "We should have left town."

"I'm sure glad you didn't," Dan said. "Grandma, Teddy, and I would still be stuck on the roof!"

FROM HURRICANES TO TORNADOES

Coastal areas aren't the only places that hurricanes can affect. When hurricanes reach land, **tornadoes** can sometimes form in the outer rain bands. Tornadoes are fast-spinning, funnel-shaped storms. Like hurricanes, they can cause a lot of damage. In 2004, Hurricane Ivan caused 127 different tornadoes to form. They occurred across nine states on the East Coast of the United States.

Tornadoes can produce winds of more than 300 miles per hour (483 kph).

No one was able to return home for months. When they finally did, there were many repairs to be made. Carrie and Dan helped fix the windows on Carrie's house.

"Perfect," said Carrie's dad. "Next time a storm hits, these should hold up better."

"Next time, can we just try to get out of town before the storm hits?" Carrie asked.

"Just make sure to pick up me, Teddy, and Grandma on your way!" Dan added with a grin.

NEW WAYS TO BUILD

Engineers and **architects** are developing ways to construct hurricane-proof buildings. Some buildings are raised above the ground where floodwaters can't reach them. Others have specially shaped roofs. This allows strong winds to blow over them without tearing the buildings apart.

This New Orleans house is raised above the ground to avoid flooding, and was built using lightweight, wind-resistant materials.

Hurricane Danger Zones

Western North
Atlantic Ocean

Eastern Pacific Ocean

Western North
Pacific Ocean

North Indian Ocean

South
Indian Ocean

North and West
Australia

South
Pacific Ocean

PROBABLE STORM PATHS

There are seven areas of the world's oceans where hurricanes and other tropical cyclones can form. These are the places where ocean waters are warmest. They are all located near the **equator**. Each area is able to form cyclones during a different part of the year. However, most of these storms never reach land.

Timeline

1900   About 8,000 people are killed in the deadliest hurricane in U.S. history, in Galveston, Texas.

1969   A record-setting 24-foot (7.3-meter) storm surge from Hurricane Camille causes huge damage along the Gulf Coast.

1992   Hurricane Andrew damages or destroys about 125,000 homes in southern Florida.

2004   Hurricane Ivan sets a record by causing 127 tornadoes over the course of three days.

2005   Hurricane Katrina strikes the Gulf Coast and floods 80 percent of New Orleans, Louisiana. The water is up to 20 feet (6.1 m) deep.

2012   Hurricane Sandy causes massive damage in several Caribbean nations, the United States, and Canada.

Words to Know

architects (AHR-ki-tekts) people who design buildings and supervise the way they are built

engineers (en-juh-NEERZ) people who are specially trained to design and build machines or large structures such as bridges and roads

equator (i-KWAY-tur) an imaginary line around the middle of Earth that is an equal distance from the North and South Poles

evacuation (i-vak-yoo-A-shuhn) the movement away from an area or building because it is dangerous there

levees (LEV-eez) banks built up near a river or other body of water to prevent flooding

meteorologists (mee-tee-uh-RAH-luh-jists) experts in the study of Earth's atmosphere

satellites (SAT-uh-lites) spacecraft that are sent into orbit around Earth, the moon, or other heavenly bodies

tornadoes (tor-NAY-dohz) violent and very destructive windstorms that appear as dark clouds shaped like funnels

Index

ABOUT THE AUTHOR

Josh Gregory is the author of more than 90 books for kids. He has written about everything from animals to technology to history. A graduate of the University of Missouri–Columbia, he currently lives in Portland, Oregon.

ABOUT THE ILLUSTRATOR

Born and raised in Los Angeles, California, Kelly Kennedy got his start in the animation business doing designs and storyboards at Nickelodeon. Since then, he's drawn and illustrated for a variety of children's books and magazines and is currently working on some of his own stories. When not drawing, he can be found working on his old cars or playing guitar in a bluegrass band.

Visit this Scholastic website for more information about hurricanes:

www.factsfornow.scholastic.com

Enter the keyword **Hurricane**